AUG 2018

D1621486

CRYPTS, TOMBS, AND SECRET ROOMS

NEWGRANGE BURIAL CHAMBER

BY ENZO GEORGE

Gareth Stevens
PUBLISHING

Please visit our website, www.garethstevens.com. For a free color catalog of all our high-quality books, call toll free 1-800-542-2595 or fax 1-877-542-2596.

Cataloging-in-Publication Data
Names: George, Enzo.
Title: Newgrange burial chamber / Enzo George.
Description: New York : Gareth Stevens Publishing, 2018. | Series: Crypts, tombs, and secret rooms | Includes index.
Identifiers: ISBN 9781538206591 (pbk.) | ISBN 9781538206539 (library bound) | ISBN 9781538206416 (6 pack)
Subjects: LCSH: Megalithic monuments--Ireland. | Tombs--Ireland. | Newgrange Site (Ireland)
Classification: LCC GN806.5 G47 2018 | DDC 936.2--dc23

Published in 2018 by
Gareth Stevens Publishing
111 East 14th Street, Suite 349
New York, NY 10003

Copyright © 2018 Gareth Stevens

For Brown Bear Books Ltd:
Managing Editor: Tim Cooke
Designer: Lynne Lennon
Editorial Director: Lindsey Lowe
Children's Publisher: Anne O'Daly
Design Manager: Keith Davis
Picture Manager: Sophie Mortimer

Picture credits:
Cover: Joe Houghton
Interior: Alamy: Jorge Tutor 19, RM Ireland 21; **Curious Ireland:** 40; **Dreamstime:** Yulika 26, Antenacamidio 39; **iStock:** 12, Richard Cano 14, Stephan Hoerold 15, Dierdre Rusk 20, UnaPhoto 23, Wedidit Media 28, Richard Semik 35; **Public Domain:** Llywelyn2000 29; **National Museum of Ireland:** 27, 30, 43; **Office of Public Works:** 5, 8, 11, 22, 24, 34, 42; **Robert Hunt Library:** 31, 32; **Shutterstock:** Rodrigo Belizzi 25, Pecoid 9, Sergii Ruduik 18, UnaPhoto 17, Sara Winter 13; **Thinkstock:** Dorling Kindersley 16, istockphoto 6, 7, 10, 36, 37, 38, 41.

All other images Brown Bear Books

Brown Bear Books has made every attempt to contact the copyright holder.
If anyone has any information please contact licensing@brownbearbooks.co.uk

All rights reserved. No part of this book may be reproduced in any form without permission from the publisher, except by a reviewer.

Printed in the United States of America
CPSIA compliance information: Batch CS17GS: For further information contact Gareth Stevens, New York, New York at 1-800-542-2595

CONTENTS

WORDS IN THE GLOSSARY APPEAR IN **BOLD** TYPE
THE FIRST TIME THEY ARE USED IN THE TEXT.

THE TOMB
BY THE RIVER

On a curve of the Boyne River north of Dublin, the capital city of Ireland, is a massive round structure made from large stones and earth. This is Newgrange, one of the oldest buildings in the world. Experts date its construction to 3200 BC, which makes the monument around 700 years older than Stonehenge in England and older than Egypt's ancient pyramids.

Built by Ireland's first farmers, Newgrange was a tomb for burying the dead. In the last 50 years, experts have discovered that it was probably also a temple. Like Stonehenge, Newgrange is **aligned** according to the position of the sun in the sky. On the winter solstice, the shortest day of the year, the rays of the rising sun enter a small hole above the entrance to the tomb and flood the central chamber of the tomb with light.

The tomb at Newgrange has been restored to how experts believe it appeared when it was first built.

STONES OF THE PAST

Newgrange is a vast structure. Its circular stone wall encloses a grassy mound about 278 feet (85 m) across and up to 44 feet (13 m) high. The entrance to the tomb is on the southeast side. A narrow, stone-lined passage 62 feet (19 m) long leads to the chamber at the heart of the monument. The passage forms one arm of the cross-shaped chamber. The other three short arms each holds a large stone basin, two of which are made of sandstone and one of **granite**.

The burial mound stands on top of a hill, and can be seen from many miles away.

The Boyne River loops around three sides of an area that includes Newgrange and other prehistoric sites.

The chamber at the center of the monument has an arched ceiling that rises 19 feet (6 m) above the floor. The unusual structure of the ceiling reflects the skill of the builders.

A BURIAL CHAMBER

Historians know little about the early farmers who lived in the valley of the Boyne River 5,000 years ago. They believe that people at the time usually cremated the dead, leaving ash and burnt bones. People buried these remains inside a tomb.

When **archaeologists** explored Newgrange, they found ash and bones in the basins of the central chamber. So far, experts have identified the remains of five individuals, but they think more people may have once been buried there.

7

Looking up at the ceiling shows how the arch is formed by using each layer of stones to support a smaller layer above it.

A SPECIAL CEILING

ARCHAEOLOGISTS BELIEVE THAT THE CEILING OF THE CENTRAL CHAMBER AT NEWGRANGE IS THE EARLIEST EXAMPLE OF A CORBELLED ROOF. THE NEOLITHIC BUILDERS FIGURED OUT HOW TO BUILD A TALL CEILING THAT WOULD NOT FALL DOWN BY CAREFULLY PLACING SMALL STONES ON TOP OF EACH OTHER SO THAT THEY GRADUALLY SLOPED INWARD IN STEPS, A TECHNIQUE CALLED CORBELLING. THE SIDES EVENTUALLY MET AT THE TOP OF THE CEILING AND WERE COVERED BY A LARGE CAPSTONE THAT HELD THE SIDES IN PLACE. THE BUILDERS WERE SO SUCCESSFUL THAT THE CEILING REMAINS SOUND AND WATERTIGHT TODAY.

PART OF A COMPLEX

Over time, experts have come to see Newgrange not as a single monument but as one of a number of important **Neolithic** sites in the valley of the Boyne. In Gaelic the valley is known as the Brú na Bóinne, or Palace of the Boyne. The site covers an area of about 1,926 acres (780 ha). It includes around 40 **passage tombs**, the largest and most elaborate of which are Newgrange, Knowth, and Dowth. The three monuments occupy prominent positions in the landscape.

The complex also includes four henges, which are circular ditches and banks surrounding circles of standing stones or wooden posts. They were probably linked to the tombs. At Knowth, builders erected a timber circle east of the main mound in around 2700 BC. Similarly, an earth henge was constructed around 2500 BC to the northeast of the tomb at Dowth. The Brú na Bóinne also includes individual standing stones and more **enclosures** marked by banks and ditches.

The passage grave at Knowth is one of the largest monuments in the Brú na Bóinne complex.

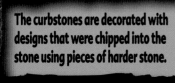
The curbstones are decorated with designs that were chipped into the stone using pieces of harder stone.

PREHISTORIC DESIGNS

At Newgrange, the base of the **retaining wall** is made up of 97 huge **curbstones**. Some are carved with spiral or diamond-shaped patterns, and other geometric designs. They were carved into the rock using stone tools. The farmers did not have metal tools. These designs are not unique to Newgrange. Similar designs have been found at other **megalithic** (large stone) sites outside Ireland.

One feature of Newgrange is unique. This is the "roof-box," a cube-shaped opening above the entrance. A section of the roof-box is covered by a square block of quartz, which seems to have been designed to move backward and forward like a shutter. On the winter solstice, the sun's rays pass through the gap in the roof-box to flood the central chamber with light. The spectacle lasts just 17 minutes before the chamber is plunged back into darkness for another year.

THE WINTER SOLSTICE

MANY ANCIENT CULTURES OBSERVED THE SUMMER AND WINTER SOLSTICES AS IMPORTANT DAYS ON THE ANNUAL RELIGIOUS CALENDAR. THE WINTER SOLSTICE OCCURS WHEN THE SUN IS AT ITS LOWEST IN THE SKY, WHICH IS NORMALLY AROUND DECEMBER 21. THE DAY IS THE SHORTEST IN THE YEAR AND THE NIGHT IS THE LONGEST. THE SUMMER SOLSTICE IS WHEN THE DAYLIGHT IS LONGEST AND THE NIGHTTIME IS SHORTEST, USUALLY AROUND JUNE 21.

The passageway at Newgrange is angled so that it is lit up by the rising sun on the winter solstice.

BUILDING THE MONUMENT

During the Neolithic period, people in Ireland lived in small farming settlements. They had no metal tools to carve stones, no wheels to transport stones, and no **mortar** to hold stones in place. The builders of Newgrange, however, had to position and carve 97 huge stones, as well as moving around 200,000 tons (181,000 t) of smaller stones to build the mound above the tomb. They had to bring stones from up to 50 miles (80 km) away and move everything uphill to the site of the monument.

Twelve large stones stand near the tomb. They were once part of a larger circle of standing stones.

Granite for the tomb was quarried in the Mourne Mountains , which can be seen in the distance from Newgrange.

A WELL-ORGANIZED WORKFORCE

Modern experts estimate that it would have taken a workforce of around 300 people between 20 and 30 years to build Newgrange. This was a huge task at a time when communities were very small and the average lifespan was only 40 years.

Experts believe that the Newgrange workforce was organized in at least six groups with different tasks. The first group had to find the large stones needed for construction. Because people lacked the tools to cut the stones, they had to find the right shape and size stone to fit the structure. Analysis shows that the quartz at Newgrange came from the Dublin–Wicklow Mountains 50 miles (80 km) away. The granite came from the Mourne Mountains to the north of Newgrange.

The second group of workers were the structural experts. They were responsible for figuring out how to make the giant curbstones around the mound stay standing upright. They also had to figure out how to position the stones to construct the **vault** in the main chamber. Each stone supported those above it as the ceiling narrowed to an arch. Most importantly, these structural workers had to figure out the exact alignment of the long passageway with the sunrise on the winter solstice. They achieved this without pencil or paper. Most likely they marked the path of the sun's rays with sticks, and then figured out the position of the passageway and the height at which to place the roof-box.

The quartz retaining wall that surrounds the monument is controversial. Some experts argue that the original covering was not as white as the restored covering.

The entrance was guarded by a huge decorated rock carved with a spiral design. It was placed across the doorway.

NEOLITHIC PEOPLES

NEWGRANGE WAS BUILT BY FARMING PEOPLES IN THE NEOLITHIC, OR NEW STONE AGE, PERIOD, WHICH LASTED FROM AROUND 10,200 BC TO AROUND 2000 BC. THE FARMERS GREW WHEAT AND BARLEY AS THEIR STAPLE CROPS. THEY ALSO ATE CARROTS, AND KEPT PIGS AND DOGS FOR THEIR MEAT. BONES FROM BOTH ANIMALS HAVE BEEN FOUND CLOSE TO NEWGRANGE. THE PEOPLE USED FLINT FOR MAKING SHARP TOOLS, KNIVES, AND WEAPONS. THEY WORSHIPED THE SUN AND BELIEVED HILLS WERE SACRED, WHICH IS WHY THEY BUILT THEIR TOMBS THERE.

This cutaway diagram shows the path of the sun's rays on the winter solstice (orange) and the corbelled arch of the central chamber.

Archaeologists believe that a third group of workers transported construction materials to the site. The largest stones each weighed several tons, and no one knows exactly how the builders moved them. They might have tied together logs to make a sled, then used the sled to drag the stones to the site. Perhaps they used the Boyne River to move the stones on rafts. Simply moving the huge stones uphill from the river to the monument would have required a lot of effort.

Experts believe another group of men cut down trees for timber. They erected wooden **scaffolding** for the builders. They also used logs for the rollers to move the stones. Other workers cut nearby **turf** into strips that they laid on top of the mound when it was built. These workers may also have been responsible for working out how to seal the joints in the stone ceiling so that the inside of the tomb stayed dry.

Finally, a group of artists and stone carvers are thought to have decorated the huge slabs with **geometric** patterns. Experts analyzing the different designs think they were created by a number of craftsmen. Some were highly skilled but others were likely apprentices still learning their craft.

HOW WAS IT BUILT?

Before the tomb could be built, the site had to be excavated by hand. Once the site had been cleared, the large stones lining the passageway — called orthostats — were maneuvered into place. They had to be precisely placed to align with the sun's rays on the winter solstice. The central chamber was also constructed at this time, with its spectacular ceiling.

The decorations at Newgrange are all abstract. The artists did not attempt to depict real objects or people.

STONE MONUMENTS

THERE ARE UP TO 200 MEGALITHIC MONUMENTS IN IRELAND. THEY ARE NOT UNIQUE. PREHISTORIC BUILDERS CONSTRUCTED TOMBS AND STONE CIRCLES IN MANY PARTS OF NORTHERN EUROPE. EXPERTS BELIEVE THE BUILDERS OF NEWGRANGE AND THE BRÚ NA BÓINNE LIKELY CAME TO IRELAND FROM BRITTANY, IN NORTHERN FRANCE. BRITTANY HAS A LARGE NUMBER OF MEGALITHIC SITES, INCLUDING A PASSAGE TOMB ON THE ISLAND OF GAVRINIS JUST OFF THE COAST.

The tomb at Gavrinis in Brittany was probably built between 4500 and 3000 BC.

The ceilings inside Newgrange are carved with spiral patterns. Such patterns also appear on other megalithic monuments, such as the Gavrinis tomb in France.

Large slabs were laid across the orthostats in the passageway to form a roof. The underside of this roof was decorated with geometric symbols before the whole tomb was then buried beneath a giant mound of earth, called a **cairn**. In order to support the huge weight of the structure, the 97 curbstones were positioned around the edge of the mound. Some experts think that the curbstones may have supported a retaining wall covered with a layer of white quartz, which would have shone in the sun. That would have made the tomb visible for miles around. The top of the mound was covered in turf, as it is today.

SECRETS OF THE PAST

Newgrange still has many secrets to reveal. Experts don't know why it was built, or whether the builders saw it primarily as a tomb or as an ancient place of worship. One of the biggest mysteries about Newgrange was solved in the 1960s. **Excavators** found an unusual stone slot above the entrance to the passageway. Over the centuries, the slot had become almost completely blocked by weeds and grass.

Some of the original standing stones (below, far right) still guard the entrance to the tomb at Newgrange.

The roof-box above the entrance is unique to Newgrange. Its existence was not discovered until the 1960s.

The Irish archaeologist Michael J. O'Kelly spent much of his working life excavating Newgrange. He thought that the entrance on the southeast side of the mound had been carefully positioned. People in the area told stories that the sun's rays shone into the tomb on the summer solstice, but O'Kelly knew that this was impossible. The entrance pointed in the wrong direction for the midsummer sun. O'Kelly wondered if the opposite was true. Might the tomb be aligned toward the winter solstice?

TESTING THE THEORY

Having come up with his theory, O'Kelly had to wait until the middle of December to test it. He visited Newgrange before dawn on the winter solstice in 1967. Luckily, it was a clear day.

The rays of the sun shine through the roof-box and along the passsageway toward the central chamber.

O'Kelly made his way down the passageway toward the central chamber, where he waited for the sun to rise. He later described the experience as the light entered the tomb:

"The light began as a thin pencil and widened to a band of about 6 inches [15 cm]. There was so much light reflected from the floor that I could walk around inside without a lamp...It was so bright that I could see the roof 20 feet [6 m] above me."

A SUN TEMPLE

O'Kelly's discovery suggested that Newgrange was no ordinary tomb. It had been built carefully so that the sun penetrated the inner chamber once a year on the winter solstice.

THE ENTRANCE STONE

MOST OF THE DECORATED STONES AT NEWGRANGE WERE CARVED BEFORE THEY WERE PUT IN PLACE. THE ONE EXCEPTION TO THIS IS THE LARGE ENTRANCE STONE POSITIONED IN FRONT OF THE DOORWAY. MEASURING 10 FEET LONG AND 4 FEET HIGH (3 X 1 M) AND WEIGHING AROUND 5.5 TONS (5 T), THE STONE WAS CARVED IN ITS PLACE. ITS FRONT IS CARVED WITH GROUPS OF THREE SPIRALS, WHICH CONTINUE ALL THE WAY TO THE BOTTOM, ALTHOUGH THERE ARE ALSO SOME BOXLIKE SHAPES. THE "TRIPLE SPIRAL" MOTIF IS REPEATED IN THE PASSAGEWAY AND THE CHAMBER. WHAT IT MEANS IS NOT KNOWN, BUT IT IS CLEAR THE CARVINGS WERE MADE BY HIGHLY SKILLED ARTISTS.

Evidence suggests that the entrance stone was only decorated after it had been put in place at the opening of the tomb.

The "triple spiral" design at Newgrange may have had a symbolic meaning, but experts do not know what it was.

O'Kelly's experience suggested that the tomb may have had another function. Prehistoric peoples often worshiped the sun, so the tomb may have had religious significance as a temple for sun worship. Alternatively, it may have reflected a belief in the **afterlife**. Perhaps the people of Newgrange believed that, when the sun's rays bathed the inner chamber, the light somehow transformed the human remains in the stone basins. Experts have many theories, or ideas, about why the sun aligned with the passageway, but they remain just theories.

WHOSE TOMB WAS IT?

The designs on the rocks and slabs might give clues about the purpose of Newgrange. They feature a variety of geometric shapes. The shapes include flowing shapes such as circles, spirals, and arcs, and straight lines such as lozenges and chevrons. There are no images of animals or people. Some experts think that the patterns were purely decorative, while others think they had a meaning that has been lost over time.

The sophisticated designs on the stones and the amount of time taken to build the monument suggest that the tomb was intended for someone important. Some experts believe it was built for a member of a royal family or someone of noble birth. But there is no direct evidence to support this theory.

Another theory is that Newgrange was a "house of the dead," where the dead could live in a similar way to the living. The builders made sure to keep the tomb dry. They carved grooves in the roof slabs so that any water that soaked through

Carved spirals also appear on some of the standing stones outside the monument.

This curbstone at Newgrange has an unusual design of parallel wavy lines, but again experts are unsure of its meaning.

the turf would run off the tomb and not into the chamber. Inside the tomb, the temperature is an even 50° Fahrenheit (10° C). Some experts have suggested that this was because the tomb was built as a dwelling place. The builders wanted to create somewhere that would be a comfortable temperature. The experts suggest that this also explains why the tomb was made from stones rather than timber and thatch, which would perish over time. The tomb was built to last.

So far, experts have identified the remains of five people in the tomb. Three had been burned, but the other two were buried as whole bodies. If unburned bodies were commonly placed in tombs, then perhaps Newgrange had been built as a home for the dead.

THE ROYAL KINGS OF TARA

IN THE PAST, SOME PEOPLE LINKED THE TOMB AT NEWGRANGE WITH ONE OF IRELAND'S LEGENDARY EARLY RULING FAMILIES, THE KINGS OF TARA. A LEGEND REPORTED THAT ONE OF THE KINGS OF TARA, CORMAC MAC AIRT, BECAME A CHRISTIAN AND REFUSED TO BE BURIED AT NEWGRANGE BECAUSE IT WAS NOT A CHRISTIAN TOMB. THIS SUGGESTED THAT NEWGRANGE WAS THE TRADITIONAL TARA TOMB, BUT IT COULD NOT HAVE BEEN. IF THE TARA KINGS EVER RULED OUTSIDE LEGEND, IT WAS 3,000 YEARS AFTER NEWGRANGE WAS BUILT.

This gold jewelry from the Bronze Age was found near Newgrange. Is it a sign that the tomb was meant for royalty?

INVESTIGATING THE PAST

Newgrange was forgotten for thousands of years. It became hidden by grass and weeds, and cows grazed on top of it. Almost 4,000 years after the tomb was built, the land on which it stands became the property of nearby Mellifont Abbey. The area around the tomb became part of the monastery's farms or granges (this is where the modern name Newgrange comes from). The monks thought the tomb was simply a mound of earth, so they did not investigate it. By 1699 the land belonged to a man named Charles Campbell. He ordered workmen to dig into the mound to find stones for construction.

When the tomb collapsed and became overgrown, cows climbed over it to graze on the top.

The workers discovered a huge boulder with strange designs carved on it. What happened next is not known for certain, but Campbell somehow discovered the entrance to the tomb. Holding a flaming torch, he became the first person to enter Newgrange for many centuries. News about the tomb's passageway and chamber soon spread.

SAVED!

The story of Campbell's discovery reached an expert on ancient buildings named Edward Lhuyd. Lhuyd hurried to the site. He was not particularly impressed with the tomb, but he did manage to persuade Campbell not to reuse the stones for construction. Lhuyd's intervention probably saved the site from destruction.

The Welshman Edward Lhuyd was a pioneer of the study of ancient monuments in Celtic areas of the British Isles, including Ireland and Scotland.

This photograph from the late 1800s shows a young visitor in the entrance before the roof-box was discovered.

Lhuyd decided that invading Vikings had built the tomb in between the 700s and the 900s. It was not until the late 1800s that another **antiquarian**, George Petrie, guessed that Newgrange had been built by early Irish farmers.

THE 20TH CENTURY

In the 1930s the first excavations began at the site. By then, cattle roamed over the mound and its sides had collapsed, burying the curbstones. In 1962, Michael J. O'Kelly started the first serious investigation of Newgrange. He and his team would work there for the next 13 years. It was O'Kelly who discovered the passageway's alignment with the winter solstice. His work was not without **controversy**, however.

A FAMOUS VISITOR

SIR WILLIAM WILDE WAS ONE OF THE MOST IMPORTANT SURGEONS IN IRELAND. HE VISITED NEWGRANGE IN 1837, AND REPORTED THAT THE SITE WAS REMARKABLE, DESPITE THE FACT THAT IT WAS OVERGROWN WITH BRAMBLES. WILDE WAS PARTICULARLY STRUCK BY THE SPIRAL CARVINGS HE SAW ON VARIOUS STONES. HE SUGGESTED THAT THEY WERE CLEARLY IMPORTANT, EVEN THOUGH HE DID NOT KNOW THEIR MEANING.

Sir William Wilde was the father of the famous Irish playwright Oscar Wilde.

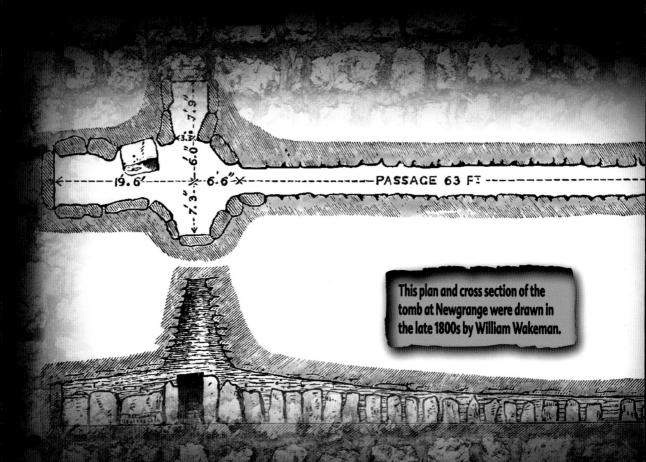

This plan and cross section of the tomb at Newgrange were drawn in the late 1800s by William Wakeman.

PASSAGE 63 FT

A CONTROVERSIAL RESTORATION

Over the centuries, the weight of the vast stone mound had caused the tomb to fall in on itself. O'Kelly took charge of restoring the structure to its original shape. He figured out the shape the mound had been to make sure the restoration was as authentic as possible. The first job was to collect the original quartz stones O'Kelly believed had been used on the façade. Then O'Kelly built a retaining wall above the curbstones using concrete and reinforced steel. This was a controversial choice. The materials are both modern, and the original builders did not have access to such technology.

Critics of O'Kelly's restoration also point out that the quartz he set into the retaining wall may not have been used for the same purpose in the original design.

DATING NEWGRANGE

IN ORDER TO ESTABLISH WHEN NEWGRANGE WAS BUILT, ARCHAEOLOGISTS USED **RADIOCARBON DATING**. THIS TECHNIQUE MEASURES THE SPEED OF DECAY OF CARBON ATOMS IN MATERIAL THAT WAS ONCE LIVING. AT NEWGRANGE, SCIENTISTS TESTED ORGANIC MATERIAL THE NEOLITHIC BUILDERS HAD USED TO PACK GAPS IN THE ROOF SLABS. THE SCIENTISTS' FINDINGS DATED NEWGRANGE TO ABOUT 3200 BC —MAKING IT OLDER THAN THE PYRAMIDS OF EGYPT OR STONEHENGE IN ENGLAND.

One critic said the restored wall was like "a cream-cheese cake with dried currants distributed about."

33

O'Kelly's critics suggested that the quartz stones might have been part of a path running outside the curbstones. As with much of Newgrange, there is no way of telling exactly how the cairn looked when it was completed 5,000 years ago. Some experts believe the builders faced the walls with shining white quartz in order to make the monument more visible. Other experts accept that the builders had indeed finished the **façade** with stones, but that these stones were not the brilliant white used by O'Kelly. Why the builders went to so much effort to quarry and transport the stones from some distance away remains a mystery.

Excavators gather pieces of white quartz from near the entrance during excavations at Newgrange in the early 1960s.

The walls beside the entrance were built during the restoration to make the tomb more accessible.

THE ROOF-BOX

In the mid-1800s, George Petrie had noted the edge of a carved stone lying above the entrance to the tomb. Petrie and later archaeologists wondered what it was for, but the mystery was not solved until the 1960s. Michael O'Kelly discovered that the stone was part of a cube-shaped opening with beautiful carvings, set at a slight angle above the entrance to the tomb, and figured out its role in admitting sunlight to the tomb during sunrise on the winter solstice.

O'Kelly's realization that there was a connection between the monument and such a key date on the calendar probably remains the most exciting of all the finds at Newgrange in the 1900s. It suggested for the first time that the site was not simply a tomb but might also have been a place of worship.

THE MONUMENT TODAY

Today, Newgrange is the most visited ancient site in Ireland. In 1993, the site was made a World Heritage site in recognition of its importance. Experts are still learning new details about its history. They now know, however, that it was built by the farming people who lived in the area at the time. In the 1800s, archaeologists regarded Ireland as being a **backwater** that would have been incapable of producing such an impressive monument. They suggested the Vikings as the most likely builders of Newgrange. Today, we know they were wrong.

The passage tombs at Knowth resemble smaller versions of the huge tomb at Newgrange.

The Boyne River valley is home to a remarkable collection of megalithic monuments.

BRÚ NA BÓINNE

Newgrange sits in an area known as the Brú na Bóinne, or "Palace of the Boyne." The area contains many Neolithic monuments, including passage tombs, henges, standing stones, and enclosures. Of more than 40 passage tombs, the three largest are Newgrange, Knowth, and Dowth.

The tombs at Newgrange and Dowth both align to the winter solstice and all three tombs are located in prominent positions. Knowth is the largest of the three tombs. It has more examples of megalithic art than Newgrange itself.

NEW DISCOVERIES

In the last 30 years, experts have discovered that Newgrange was not completed in the Neolithic period. Later builders erected 12 standing stones in a circle at a distance from the mound. Archaeologists used radiocarbon dating to discover the age of the stones. They believe that the stone circle was built about 1,000 years after the tomb, during the Bronze Age. They also think that the circle originally contained as many as 37 stones. The purpose of the stones is unclear.

In 1982, workers began digging foundations for a new tourist guide hut in the far southeastern corner of the site at Newgrange. They stumbled across a series of buried pits that had been dug and filled back in. Each pit had measured around 3 to 4 feet (1–1.2 m) across and about 3 to 4 feet (1–1.2 m) deep. They held nothing but animal bones and flint. Archaeologists think the pits are the same age as the mound. There is no evidence that later inhabitants of the site used them.

The standing stones in front of the entrance align with the sunrise on significant days of the calendar.

This is a reconstruction of a woodhenge that once stood at Knowth, near Newgrange.

MEGALITHIC HENGES

HENGES ARE ROUND MONUMENTS MADE UP OF WOODEN POLES OR STANDING STONES. THEY TAKE THEIR NAME FROM STONEHENGE. STONEHENGE MEANS "THE HANGING STONES," A REFERENCE TO THE STONE LINTELS, OR STRUCTURAL BLOCKS, LAID ON TOP OF THE UPRIGHTS, BUT TODAY THE NAME IS USED FOR ANY CIRCLE OF POSTS. WOODHENGES AND STONEHENGES WERE COMMON, AND CIRCLE PATTERNS OFTEN OCCUR AT PREHISTORIC SITES. EXPERTS BELIEVE THEY HAD A RELIGIOUS SIGNIFICANCE. THE MONUMENT AT STONEHENGE, FOR EXAMPLE, IS ALIGNED WITH THE POSITION OF SUNRISE ON THE SUMMER SOLSTICE.

WOODHENGE

Archaeologists made another discovery near the pits in 1982. They found a large woodhenge, or circle of posts. Nothing remains of the posts themselves, but the experts used radiocarbon dating to learn the age of the holes in which the posts once stood. The wooden circle dates from the early Bronze Age, about 4,000 years ago. It is older than the stone circle. The wooden circle is important because experts think it suggests that the people at Newgrange were changing their beliefs. They may have moved away from hidden **rituals** inside the tomb to celebrate larger ceremonies held outside in the woodhenge.

AN OBSERVATORY?

After the stone circle was built, it replaced the woodhenge as a site for ceremonies. These rituals probably involved feasting and drinking, and the **sacrifice** of animals such as pigs. The stone circle was the last structure to be built at Newgrange by people who worshipped the sun. Archaeologists have discovered that some of the standing stones align with the sun and the stone in front of the tomb.

The Beaker People are named for the pottery vessels they made. They arrived at Newgrange sometime after the monument was built.

Passage graves are named for the central passage that led to the burial chamber. At Newgrange, the stone-lined passage is 62 feet (19 m) long.

On the shortest day of the year, the sun casts the shadow of one of the surviving standing stones onto the entrance stone at Newgrange. During the spring and fall equinoxes, the two days a year when the day and night are of equal length, the shadow cast by the second stone to the east strikes the entrance stone. At the summer solstice, the rising sun forms a line with the three surviving stones in front of the entrance stone to mark the longest day of the year. Could it be that the stone circle had a ceremonial and religious function for the farmers who built it? Perhaps the moving shadows of the stones helped them divide the year so they knew when to plant their crops and when to harvest them.

A LOTTERY

NEWGRANGE IS ONE OF THE MOST POPULAR ANCIENT TOURIST DESTINATIONS IN IRELAND. THIS CAUSES A PROBLEM EACH WINTER SOLSTICE. SO MANY PEOPLE WANT TO WITNESS THE REMARKABLE SPECTACLE OF THE TOMB FILLING WITH LIGHT THAT THE ONLY WAY TO OBTAIN TICKETS IS THROUGH A LOTTERY. EACH YEAR, THE VISITORS' CENTER AT NEWGRANGE RUNS A LOTTERY, AND AROUND 30,000 PEOPLE ENTER TO BE ONE OF 60 WINNERS THAT GET TO BRING ONE GUEST AND SEE THE TOMB FILL WITH LIGHT. EVEN THOSE LUCKY ENOUGH TO WIN A TICKET CANNOT BE CERTAIN THAT THE SKIES WILL BE CLEAR ENOUGH FOR A VISIBLE SUNRISE.

Up to 200,000 visitors come to Newgrange every year, making it Ireland's leading archaeological site.

WHAT BECAME OF NEWGRANGE?

Archaeologists are 95 percent certain that no ceremonies or burials took place at Newgrange after about 2045 BC. Later, however, Newgrange became a popular **pilgrimage** site. The Celts arrived in Ireland from Europe in around 500 BC. They saw Newgrange as a special place. The mound features in many of their **myths** as the home of their gods. The Romans also visited Newgrange in the early centuries AD. Gold coins and jewelry found during excavations of the mound have been dated to as late as AD 400.

After that, Newgrange was all but forgotten until it was rediscovered by Charles Campbell in 1699. Since then, it has puzzled and fascinated experts and amateurs alike for hundreds of years.

Gold coins found at Newgrange suggest that the Romans visited the site during their occupation of Britain.

TIMELINE

BC

c.4500 The passage tomb at Gavrinis in Brittany is built sometime after this.

c.3200 The tomb at Newgrange is built around now. The nearby monuments at Dowth and Knowth may have been built at around the same period.

c.2700 Builders at Knowth erect a timber circle near the tomb.

c.2500 An earth henge, or circular enclosure, is built near the tomb at Dowth.

c.2500 A people known as the Beaker People arrive in Ireland, probably from England. They are named for the pottery vessels they made.

c.2200 A stone circle and wooden circle are built at Newgrange. They may be evidence of a change in the people's beliefs and worship.

2045 The last burials take place in the tomb at Newgrange.

500s The Celtic people arrive in Ireland from central Europe. They adopt Newgrange into their own mythology.

AD

1699   Charles Campbell, the owner of the land at Newgrange, discovers the tomb when his workers open the mound looking for stone for construction.

1830s   The Irish antiquarian and artist George Petrie discovers the roof-box at Newgrange.

1837   Surgeon Sir William Wilde visits Newgrange and notes the remarkable carvings on the large stones.

1930s   The first excavations take place at the site.

1962   Professor Michael J. O'Kelly begins 13 years of excavations at Newgrange.

1963   O'Kelly establishes the link between the roof-box and the winter solstice, revolutionizing understanding of the monument and its purpose.

1993   The Newgrange Burial Chamber is added to the UNESCO list of World Heritage sites.

GLOSSARY

afterlife An existence enjoyed by the dead after they die.

aligned Placed to form a straight line.

antiquarian Someone who studies and collects old books and objects.

archaeologists People who study history by examining old structures and artifacts.

backwater A place of little importance or progress.

cairn A mound of stones.

controversy A long public disagreement or debate.

curbstones Long narrow stones arranged to form a kerb, or raised barrier.

enclosures Areas that are surrounded by barriers, such as ditches or banks.

excavators People who carefully uncover buried sites or objects.

façade The decorated front of a building.

geometric Describes a pattern with regular lines and shapes.

granite A very hard rock often used in construction.

megalithic Relating to ancient monuments built with large stones, or megaliths.

mortar A mixture of sand and cement used in construction.

myths Traditional stories about the gods and origins of a people.

Neolithic Relating to the Late Stone Age, from about 10,200 to 2000 BC.

passage tombs Ancient tombs with a narrow passage made with large stones covered in earth.

pilgrimage A journey made to a sacred site for religious purposes.

radiocarbon dating A method of dating objects by measuring the decay of a type of carbon atom.

retaining wall A wall built to hold back earth.

rituals Solemn religious ceremonies.

sacrifice Making an offering to the gods.

scaffolding A framework of poles used during construction.

turf A layer of grass and soil.

vault A roof in the form of an arch.

FURTHER INFORMATION

Books

Francis, Paul.
Newgrange and Brú na Bóinne. Ireland's Built Heritage. Charial Publishing, 2014.

Green, Jen.
Ancient Celts. National Geographic Investigates. Washington, DC: National Geographic Children's Books, 2008.

McQuinn, Anna.
Ireland. Countries of the World. Washington, DC: National Geographic Children's Book, 2008.

Mason, Paul.
The Mystery of the Stone Circles. Can Science Solve? Chicago: Heinemann-Raintree Library, 2008.

Websites

www.newgrange.com/
The official Newgrange website, with detailed information about the monument.

www.mythicalireland.com/ ancientsites/newgrange- facts/printer-friendly.html
A printable list of 101 fascinating facts about Newgrange.

www.worldheritageireland. ie/bru-na-boinne/built -heritage/newgrange/
Detailed information about the monument and its features.

Publisher's note to educators and parents: Our editors have carefully reviewed these websites to ensure that they are suitable for students. Many websites change frequently, however, and we cannot guarantee that a site's future contents will continue to meet our high standards of quality and educational value. Be advised that students should be closely supervised whenever they access the Internet.

INDEX